Charles P. Clever

New Mexico

Resources, Necessities For Railroad Communication

Charles P. Clever

New Mexico
Resources, Necessities For Railroad Communication

ISBN/EAN: 9783744694001

Printed in Europe, USA, Canada, Australia, Japan

Cover: Foto ©ninafisch / pixelio.de

More available books at **www.hansebooks.com**

HER RESOURCES; HER NECESSITIES FOR RAILROAD
COMMUNICATION WITH THE ATLANTIC AND
PACIFIC STATES; HER GREAT FUTURE.

By CHARLES P. CLEVER,

DELEGATE FROM NEW MEXICO.

WASHINGTON, D. C.
McGILL & WITHEROW, PRINTERS AND STEREOTYPERS.
1868.

New Mexico.

HOUSE OF REPRESENTATIVES,
WASHINGTON, D. C.,
January 8, 1868.

I am so often written to and questioned about New Mexico, the Territory from which I have been returned as Delegate, that I have considered it best to have printed such *general* information about that country, and its resources, as a few hours, snatched from those occupied by the duties of my position, permit me to give.

In the sixteenth century, not long after the conquest of Mexico, an expedition was fitted out in Culiacan to proceed northward and eastward in search of the "Seven cities of Cibola," one of which was Quivira, where rumor said that gold abounded in great quantities. This rumor had been brought by some two or three persons, one a negro, who either had voluntarily wandered into that country of Cibola, or had been forcibly carried there, and had afterwards made their way back to their friends, the Spaniards. The expedition was commanded by Vasquez de Coronada, and, though small, was made up of many who belonged to the chivalry of Spain. It would be pleasant to trace out the route and the adventures of this body of those gallant and hardy spirits from the day they set out until their return; but the limits of this slight sketch do not permit this. A journal was kept by one Casteñada, who belonged to the expedition, and this has been published, and will be read with interest by all who seek to know of the early expeditions made by Europeans into the heart of our country.

When the people belonging to Coronada's expedition returned to the settled portions of the vice royalty of Mexico, they imparted to their countrymen there a knowledge of the beautiful and salubrious region they had visited. Settlers began to migrate northward toward Sonora and Chihuahua, and finally into New Mexico. This was early in the seventeenth century. Farms were then opened, and large churches were built by Indian labor under the direction of Catholic missionaries; and, tradition says, that rich .mines were discovered, in which the Indians were compelled by force, and often by cruelty, to toil. At length, exasperated beyond further endurance, they rose on their oppressors, and destroying many, drove all of the remainder out of New Mexico as far southward as El Paso del Norte. This was in the month of August, in the year 1680.

About twenty years afterwards, a new effort was made by the Spaniards to settle the country. This was permanently successful; but the new comers for a long time never ventured far from the valley of the Rio Grande. Back from that river, away amidst the mountains, and on the plains, are still seen the ruins of churches and monasteries which, as ruins, excite admiration; and, from their remoteness, grandeur, and now utter loneliness, are subjects of wonder and curious speculation. As they now interest the antiquary and the ethnologist, so when time slips away, and the Scotts and Schillers, and Byrons and Longfellows come there, then they will be rebuilt and repeopled, and be known in enduring song. The very veil of mystery which seems now to hang about them, and about those who built them, will be apparently rent away, and what is now but so lonely and so weird, will then be made bright and enchanting forever.

Since the Territory of Arizona was set off from New Mexico, the latter Territory extends from longitude 103° to longitude 109°, west from Greenwich; and from latitude 31° 30′ to latitude 37° north, and contains 121,201 square miles, or 77,568,640 acres. The Rio Grande and the Pecos river are the principal rivers, which run through it from a northerly to a southerly direction. The streams forming the head-waters of the Canadian affluent to the Arkansas, are those draining the eastern side of the Territory. Cordilleras of the Rocky Mountains run from north to south, but are here and there lost in the table lands to rise again further on, either as isolated peaks, or as short sierras. From the most eastern of these ranges, and extending toward the east, are vast *steppes*, like terraces, one lower than the other, marking ancient levels of the country, the summits of which gradually slope toward the Mississippi. Through these steppes during the lapse of *eons* of ages, the rivers and streams have worn for themselves channels, and grooved out valleys of the most surpassing loveliness and of great fertility. The valley of the Rio Grande and of the Pecos have been fashioned in the same manner, and are intervales of like character; but near the head of the Pecos, and on each side of the upper Rio Grande, the country rises into mountain peaks of indescribable grandeur and beauty.

West of the Rio Grande lies a country of table lands, or *mesas*, with broad valleys between. These *mesas* are also the remains of a former level, and many of them, standing out apart from others, resemble fortresses and castles of a size sufficient to have been occupied by armies of Titans. Here and there, amongst them, rises up a peak, now become an extinct volcano. Down the side of these peaks, and over some of the mesas I have described, and through valleys between mesas, once poured rivers of lava. Even now, as the traveller comes to some of these rivers, they seem as if they must have been suddenly arrested in their course, and been cooled only a few years gone by into black and immovable stone.

In the southwestern portion of the Territory there is a range of high mountains extending from the Rio Grande far into Arizona. The waters running off their southern slope form the head-waters of the Miembres, which runs toward Lake Guzman, in Chihuahua; and also form the head-waters of the Gila, running westward into the Colorado.

The mountains throughout New Mexico are clad with forests of pine, spruce, cedar, fir, and other kindred trees. At high altitudes the aspen is found in great quantities. The foot hills and many of the mesas, are covered with the piñon, often intermixed with cedar trees. Along the rivers and streams, the natural growth is principally made up of cottonwoods, sycamores, hackberry, willow, wild grape vines, &c. On streams in the southern part of the country, walnut and oak are found; but not to any great extent. The *whole* of New Mexico may be said to be covered with grass; for even in the forests is found the year around the most luxuriant grass. In the winter time, at very great altitudes, this grass is covered with snow; but it does not seem to be killed to the ground, for as soon as the snow melts, it at once affords excellent grazing. All over the mesas and through the valleys, grows the *grama*, a grass justly celebrated for its nutritious qualities. This does not wilt and become efféte in winter; but becomes cured as hay, just where it stands, and the flocks and herds feed upon it all winter. It may here be said, that New Mexico is so delightfully situated as to climate, that, as a pastoral region, its grazing is not destroyed by the cold storms and bleaching rains of the countries farther north; nor is it burnt up or become stunted and sparse, by the burning heats of the countries further south.

The valleys of the rivers can all be successfully cultivated. The cultivation of land in New Mexico is mainly by the help of irrigation. It is true, it costs some labor to make the ditches, but, then, the farmer is sure of a crop; and the running over his land of water highly charged with detritus, made up of decayed vegetation and rich mould from the mountains above, is a source of fertility. In this way the land never wears out. Irrigation thus becomes a fertilizer.

The agricultural interests of New Mexico have heretofore been confined to the raising of wheat, corn, beans, oats, barley. In some localities in the north, potatoes grow well; but along the valleys they cannot be successfully cultivated. The *chile*, or red pepper, of which the Spanish people make some fine dishes, is grown in great abundance all over the country. Since the Americans have gone to New Mexico, nearly all kinds of garden vegetables and fruits have been introduced, and grow luxuriously and are of excellent size and flavor. Peaches, apples, apricots, grapes, and in the south, quinces, pomegranates and figs, can be grown as well in New Mexico as in any part of the world. Indeed, with such a variety of climate, and with such a rich and varied soil, it is difficult to conceive of any kind of fruit, except that which needs the fervor of a tropical sun, that could not be grown within the boundaries of New Mexico. The variety of the grape which is most cultivated in New Mexico, cannot be surpassed for flavor by any grape in the world. The wine made from it far surpasses the best Burgundy. It requires but little labor to cultivate the vine, as no trellises are used. In a few years the grape culture will be one of the greatest and most profitable branches of industry in that country.

The pastoral interests will be of the next greater value. As before remarked, the *whole* country is a grazing country.

Those who raise sheep and goats know that they want a plenty of room and air. Half of the diseases incident to these animals arise from having them huddled together in yards or barns in cold weather. In New Mexico, the range is so extensive the flocks can spread out, and can move over different pasturage every successive day. No shelter is needed in the winter time. In very cold weather the flocks move southward, and when inclement storms come on go down from the uplands to seek the genial shelter of some neighboring cañon. So, except to make a start in procuring a flock of sheep or of goats, the cost of feeding and of attending them, is a mere nominal sum. As soon as we can introduce, by railroad, improved breeds of sheep, and the Cashmere goat, we can compete with the world in the production of fine wool, and of the exceedingly fine hair of that goat. Of course, what is said of the facility and cheapness of raising sheep and goats, will equally apply to the raising of horses and cattle. We can therefore furnish the best of beef, and of butter and cheese, *cheaper*, when once we are protected in the raising of stock from Indian depredations, than any country in the world. Except for work, cattle and horses, which are kept about the farms or foi daily use, hardly any hay, or fodder, or corn need be put up. The time is not far distant when our hills and mountains will literally be covered with flocks and herds.

The mineral wealth of the country is simply enormous. The almost daily discoveries of new lodes of gold and silver-bearing quartz, and of auriferous *placers*, have ceased to be a surprise in New Mexico. The people of intelligence and knowledge of such matters, *know* that as soon as men with capital can come and see what *they* see, then these mines will yield untold millions.

New Mexico has her useful metals and minerals in the greatest abundance.

I take the liberty of making some extracts from a very able report on this subject, made in 1865, by Professor Richard Dale Owen, and by Professor E. T. Cox, both gentlemen of great authority in the scientific world as geologists and chemists. The report alluded to was published in this city by the Hon. John S. Watts, formerly Delegate from New Mexico, who has labored hard to bring to public notice the value of that Territory:

"When, by a gradual ascent over the Plains, we reach the foot of the Rocky mountains we do not find a vast succession of promiscuously piled mountains; but we have several parallel ridges of crystaline rocks with sedimentary strata on their flanks, and a second series of hypogene parallel ridges with a trend diverging often 50° or more from the former; this latter also sometimes further modifying the aqueous beds. These together constitute the main dividing range which separates the waters of the great Mississippi valley from those which flow into the Pacific, while mesas or table lands, formed by the overflow of volcanic rocks, have to great extent levelled the intervening inequalities.

"In the Raton mountain, close to the stage road, we examined a five-foot bed of bituminous coal, and on reaching the summit found fossil angiospermous dicotyledonous leaves in shale of Cretaceous age. At the fine hacienda of Mr. Maxwell, formerly hunter and guide in Fremont's expedition, the proprietor pointed to his coal bed in the mountain side, distinctly visible from the house, above aluminous shales. Two miles N. E. of Santa Fé, we found a thin bed of coal, coal plants, and carboniferous limestone.

"Near the Placer mountain we examined a bed almost five feet thick of the best anthracite, altered by porphyritic contact; the same porphyry dike five miles from there, in the gold diggings of Placer, bringing up almost to a vertical position the carboniferous limestone and superincumbent sandstone, again forming a breccia near the junction; the whole overlaid by cretaceous, judging from the fragments of silicious coniferous wood, the same as seen at Galisteo creek. Lieutenant Simpson, in his expedition with Colonel Washington, found bituminous coal abundant on the Rio Puerco; and General Carleton observed a bed on Rabbit Ear creek. Coal is also dug near Fort Craig, and we heard of it in other parts of southern New Mexico.

"For convenience of reference, details will be given—1, of gold mines; 2, of silver; 3, of copper; 4, of iron and other metallic ores; 5, of mineral products not metallic.

"1. *Gold mines.*

"A. Old Placer mine, in Placer mountain, twenty-seven miles S. S. E. from Santa Fé. The mountain is situated about the point of intersection for the Jemez range, if not interrupted by the Rio Grande, with the prolongation of the Rocky mountain range, which passes east of Santa Fé, the main mass being a felspathic syenite, the summit estimated at about 8,000 feet high; but the mountain slope cut through, at less than 7,000 feet above the ocean, by a N. N. E. porphyritic dike, which, in its eruption, has brought carboniferous strata to the surface. As the name indicates, these old *placer* diggings were worked by washing the soil, although undoubtedly many auriferous sands cannot be traced to their origin, yet here, by ascending higher to the vein which furnished the gold detritus, a quartz rock is quarried and

2

brought down to the mill to be worked. The highest, or Ortiz vein, by my barometer, 6,950 feet above the sea, has been reached by shafts at numerous openings, which show that the vein trends chiefly E. of N., although two northerly openings bear somewhat west. The deepest shaft, affording the best ore, has reached a depth of over 150 feet, and when carried further down, may be expected to develop ore of greater value. The ladders being decayed, we could not descend that shaft, but by an inspection of others, and of the ore thrown out at the deep shaft, we ascertained that the wall rock is highly felspathic, and contains much iron, the vein is from one to four feet wide, and the gangue a porous drusy ferruginous quartz.

"Here, as in California, it is considered more favorable to find gold in rocks, where it is *not* visible to the naked eye, than to find occasional rich lumps, the latter being in pockets and giving out sooner, while the minutely diffused is persistent. Such is the character of the quartz vein in the Ortiz mine, particularly of those pieces having a porous ferruginous appearance.

"A short distance from this mine extensive works have been erected, a reservoir has been constructed across the outflow from a spring so as to save the water; a steam engine of forty-horse power drives the quartz crushers, besides giving motion to an arastra (or circular bed often made of phorphyry blocks) which was nearly completed when we were there, on which the crushed ore is more minutely pulverized and intimately amalgamated. On the old inferior method, we learn that for several years the average from this mine was sufficient to remunerate those engaged in it; and it is anticipated that on the more improved plan, now being introduced, much more will be realized; as formerly, the dirt which had been run off and rejected, was made to afford profit by rewashing. The annual yield, we learn, has resulted as high as $40,000 to $50,000; even according to Gregg, in his 'Commerce of the Praries,' to $80,000 in the years 1832 and 1835.

"The Cuningham works are a short distance further east,

in the same mountain where the porphyritic trap described in the general geology, has brought up and formed a breccia with a carboniferous limestone, and at other places with the overlying sandstone. The same breccia may be found yet higher toward the Ortiz openings, wherever the porphyry protrudes. At the Cuningham excavations the dike is fifty to sixty feet wide, and as the feldspar is decomposing, this brecciated rock is easily worked for gold and made profitable, although affording a lower percentage of metal than the Ortiz and adjoining Tunica quartz veins.

The ore from the Ortiz mine, after being crushed and pulverized, and after being separated from the rock and magnetic iron ore, afforded on digestion with nitric acid and being freed from impurities, a quantity* equal to three ounces and two pennyweights of gold to the ton of 2,000 pounds of the ore. This, at the present value of the metal, worth in paper money from $36 to $40 per ounce would consequently be considerably over $100 to the ton; a very heavy percentage when we consider, as already stated, that in California, companies with suitable machinery, work profitably ore affording $20 a ton or even sometimes that which realizes only $10 per ton.

"B. Gold in quartz veins near San José copper mine. Not more than a mile or at most a mile and a half west of the San José copper mine, we saw at least six parallel quartz veins, some of which had been extensively and profitably worked for gold until the miners were driven off by the Indians. The veins run somewhat E. of N. and W. of S. across a porphyritic ridge, which in its W. of N. course has tilted the sandstone with an easterly dip. From these works samples were also taken for examination and analysis. Specimens of gold quartz from many other localities were

---

*Since the above, Mr. Cox has forwarded an analysis of the gold, &c., thus obtained from the Ortiz gold quartz in the Placer mountain.
The result afforded : Gold, 99.170
      Silver, .782
      Iridium, .048
        ————
        100.000

brought us for inspection, chiefly by soldiers, affording strong evidence of the mineral wealth both of New Mexico and Arizona; but we deem it best to confine our detailed report to those regions which we visited personally, mentioning only casually such as, from the testimony of others, might merit future attention. Regarding the various modes of working these gold ores, it may not be improper to add that Ure's recommendation, based chiefly, however, on the experience obtained in European and South American gold mines, is not to melt directly with lead, (as has been proposed by some connected with the Placer,) unless the ore is remarkably rich. He adds: 'These processes are little practiced, because they are less economical than amalgamation.'

"C. We heard of gold in placer diggings twenty-five or thirty miles north of Fort Stanton, but had no opportunity of examining the locality.

"2. *Silver mines.*—The chief localities furnishing this precious metal, which we had an opportunity to visit, exhibit the silver in combination with lead. In most instances an approximate result was readily obtained, through cupellation on a small scale, under the flame of the blowpipe. The ores will, however, all be subjected to rigid analysis for exact quantitative determination.

"A. The San Adelia and Stevenson mine in Organ mountain. These are so near each other, as you are aware, (being perhaps two miles apart in a direct line in the same range,) that they may be described under one head, although owned separately.

"The Organ mountain, as far up as we examined it, is composed of a granitic porphyry, which in its protrusion has elevated not only the sandstone several hundred feet on its western slope, but has even brought up the carboniferous limestone. This occurs especially near the San Adelia mine, where the limestone is metamorphosed in places to a beautiful white chrystaline marble. Several parallel quartz veins have also cut through in a northerly and southerly direction, and it is in these the metal chiefly occurs. The Stevenson mine has been extensively worked, chiefly for the argentiferous galena, at five separate openings, each having a distinctive name. This ore afforded a good globule of silver when cupelled under the blow-pipe; but it will be further tested on a larger scale. Some openings, however, are worked for their copper ores, vitreous copper, malachite and azurite, occasionally associated with calcspar, at other times having a gangue of baryta. The amount of silver lead ore seems large, as the vein or lode frequently is five to six feet wide, never less than two feet, with the ore diffused pretty well through it. The highest opening, called San Domingo, near the summit of the uptilted sandstone, is about 1,400 feet above Las Cruces; the mesa itself at the foot of the mines being about six hundred feet above the town, and fifteen or sixteen miles distant from it. Extending for half a mile or more from the flanks of the Organ mountain, near those mines, are interesting moraines, or lines at regular intervals, of deposited boulders, chiefly porphyritic, the red variety more decomposed than the grey. B. We did not personally examine any other silver mines; but we received specimens of argentiferous galena from Pinos Altos, Apache Pass, and Stone Corral, all of which silver lead, judging from the blow-pipe examinations, would afford remunerative quantities of silver, provided the ore is as abundant as represented.

"3. *Copper mines.*

"A. *Hanover* Copper Mine.

"To reach this region from Mesilla by way of Fort Cummings, the road past the Miembres river, hot springs, and Santa Rita, is about one hundred and ten miles; but it is only ninety miles from Fort Craig to the Hanover mines, by a direct S. W. route practicable for wagons. The Hanover mines are situated about 6,350 feet above the ocean, where a syenetic granite, having large hexagonal crystals of mica, has elevated the carboniferous limestone two hundred feet up the west flank of the mountain; but the openings, of which there are many, are near the first appearance of the aqueous rock in the narrow valley, in which also the furnace is erected.

The granitic range has a strike W. of N., and bringing the
limestone up in that direction, gives it on the W. flank, a
W. of S. dip. This axis is crossed by a highly ferruginous
rock, sometimes a pure magnetic iron ore, trending apparently rather in dike form E. of N., and forming frequently
in places with the adjacent aqueous rock, for a considerable
distance, immense masses of breccia. Near these disturbing
forces a sixty-three feet shaft has been sunk, and various
tunnels run, exposing extensive deposits of copper, often
green or blue carbonate, sometimes native copper in the decomposing feldspar of the granite; occasionally (especially at
the openings down the valley from the furnace) as vitreous
copper, sometimes as grey copper. An analysis of this malachite or green carbonate of copper, has been forwarded by
Mr. Cox since the above was written. The result was, oxide
of copper 72.64=58 per cent. of metallic copper. The ore
occurs ramifying, sometimes for fifty or sixty feet in width,
through the decomposing feldspar, forms therein rich deposits
and extends vertically below any point yet reached. In some
places, where the iron ore described above intersects, it forms
the gangue, but is easily detached mechanically.

"The smelting, from all that we saw and could learn from
Mr. Hinkel, the former proprietor, now involves much less
labor and expense than is common in Europe. This gentleman had studied metallurgy in his native country, Saxony,
and had erected extensive works, which were paying well,
when he was driven off by the Indians, and compelled by
his extensive losses to sell out most of his interest in said
mines. Much of the machinery remains there, and the furnaces are standing. He ran the mixed ores first through
high, narrow furnaces, and completed the work in those of
a reverberatory form, running the metal into iron moulds,
which were procured at a cost of six hundred dollars, and
which we saw still undisturbed at the time of our visit.

"In Germany it was not unusual, some years since, to roast
for many months, and then to submit the copper to at least
five distinct smeltings; a labor rendered unnecessary at these
mines in consequence of the purity of the ore.

"The copper thus shipped to the States has commanded, ever since it was tried, a ready market at a price equal to that of the best Russia copper. It is said to be a trifle harder than that of Santa Rita, hence more suitable for nails, bolt heads, and similar work in sheathing vessels.

"This is probaly due to a slight admixture of iron, not eliminated in the imperfect mode of smelting adopted, until better machinery was obtained. The necessary materials had been purchased, and the improvements were in process of construction, when the Indian troubles commenced.

" On the hills and mountains around the Hanover furnace there is abundant timber for charcoal and fuel; pines, piñon, some walnut, and a good deal of oak. The sandstone, already mentioned, is in places suitable for furnace hearthstones; the syenite, when porphyritic, we observed to be very durable, especially that of a grey color, at least as far as we could judge from the weathering; and the limestone remote from the locality, in which its condition was, as already described, highly metamorphosed, will readily burn into lime. Water is unfailing from some springs, and is in sufficient quantity for the purposes of washing the ore, by constructing a short race or aqueduct (acequia), and thus obtaining additional force. Gramma grass, somewhat lower in the valley, is of the finest quality anywhere seen during our explorations; it was over two feet high, and would cut two tons of hay to the acre, when we were there—October 23, 1864.

" B. *Santa Rita* mines.

"These are situated on the same range, a few miles further south, and about three hundred and fifty feet lower than the Hanover furnace. The ore is of a similar character, and has been profitably worked for many years, probably for two centuries, by Spaniards and Mexicans. The native copper, which is as pure as that of Lake Superior, is washed out from the decomposing feldspar, and smelted with the malachite and azurite.

"Besides many tons of ore abandoned here, when the workmen were driven off by the Indians, we noticed much valuable machinery, including the latest improvement for obtaining the blast.

"It seems highly probable that good copper ore could be found abundantly, not only along the entire distance between Hanover and Santa Rita, but also from the indications, in some of the parallel ridges; and even in the prolongation of the Santa Rita range to San José, the next which we proceed to describe.

"C. *San Jose* Mines.

" These are 150 feet lower than the Santa Rita mines, and somewhat west of south of them. The ore, however, is still nearly of the same character, and very abundant. It occurs chiefly where quartz veins, bearing E. of N., cut through the W. of N. porphyritic range. The malachite and azurite predominate here.

"D. *Jemez* Copper Mines.

"From this locality, which is situated about fifty miles west of Santa Fé, about 1,100 pounds of ore were obtained for transportation to the States in order to be fairly tested on a large scale. The ore is chiefly vitreous copper, often coated with malachite.*

"Although snow had already fallen to a considerable extent, we found time, after completing our other work, to visit this locality. We observed the copper in sheets under heavy beds of sandstone, at an elevation of about 6,000 feet above the ocean in the northern part of the cañon of San Diego.

"4. *Iron and other metallic ores.*

"A. At the Hanover copper mines there is an inexhaustable supply of good iron ore, partly magnetic, partly a red hematite, apparently in a continuous ridge, trending towards a reported iron mountain, about fifteen miles distant, which has already been mentioned as having been examined by Captain Whitlock. At the Placer mountain, twenty-seven miles south of Santa Fé, we found also a considerable amount

---

*Since the above was written, Mr. Cox has forwarded the result of his examination of this ore, on a small scale, while awaiting the arrival of the boxes. The virteous copper afforded 60 per cent. of metallic copper.

of good iron ore, such as would probably justify the erection
of a Catalan Forge—owners of mills and others requiring
small jobs, having at present to send to the States for their
castings and other heavy job work in iron. The whole
country afforded evidence of abundant deposits of this useful metal, but that at the Placer, if sufficiently abundant, as
it appeared to be, would prove especially valuable on account
of its proximity to good anthracite coal, only six miles distant. That fuel would serve to generate steam and give,
if desired, impetus to a forge-hammer and other machinery,
which might be connected with the iron works as well as
to the quartz crushing and grinding apparatus for the gold
ore.   *   *   *

"C. *Kaolin*, or Decomposed Feldspar.

"About two miles in a direct line southerly from the San
José copper mines, we found a layer of beautifully white' and
decomposing feldspar, in the porphyritic granite, sufficient
to supply many works for years with the best material for
porcelain. The bed averages about four feet in thickness,
and was traced laterally two hundred yards and upwards.
Apparently it extends entirely through the mountain, and
the decomposition is probably the result of metamorphism.
This kaolin much resembles the deposit in Arkansas, fully
described in the State Geological Report. Other localities
were observed in which the feldspar of the granitic rocks had
thoroughly decomposed, but none were so purely white as
the above.

"The climate is so unsurpassed that if there were no other
inducement to immigration into that territory, many who, as
soldiers or travellers, have once experienced its delights,
would scarcely be satisfied elsewhere afterwards. The light,
dry, electrical atmosphere, gives a zest to mere existence,
irrespective of any other source of enjoyment, seldom if
ever experienced, I think, in any but climates of a similar
character, such as Mexico and southern California.

"The country needs only a railroad to develop its capa-
bilities. That could, for the most part of the route, be constructed at a very low cost per mile, as there would be very

2

little cutting and filling, scarcely any important culverts or bridges until we reach the mountains. Even then, by adopting the Cimarron route, the Raton Pass is avoided, and on arriving at the dividing ridge we can surmount the pass by way of Pigion's ranch along a gradual ascent from near the Pecos of not over 600 feet in ten miles. Usually this slope could be obtained without much blasting, as far as I could judge by a passing survey, but should this or even tunneling be rendered necessary, the granitic rocks of that summit are by no means very refractory. The further route, either by the 35th or 32d parallel, is well known from the Pacific railroad surveys, to encounter no serious difficulties. By having it connect near Bent's old fort, with the northern route passing near Pike's Peak, cross the Rocky Mountains between Santa Fé and Albuquerque, and pursue either of the parallels above indicated, the railroad would pass through the rich mineral regions of New Mexico and Arizona, and reach the Pacific amid. the rich cotton and vine portions of California.

"The amount of energy, enterprise, and wealth, which would thus be developed, can scarcely be over estimated. Mention has already been made of the abundant supply of coal which could be obtained along this route; and by following the river courses from bend to bend, which would require no great deviation from a direct line, the supply of water would be equally favorable.

"The climate, the immense mineral wealth and facility for making money, the chances for speculation and the good profit by taking Government contracts, by freighting, merchandising, ranching, owning stock, cultivating vineyards, and the like, will no doubt continue to make this territory, as it already is, a favorite resort for those desiring to better their condition in health or wealth."

Since the report was published, from which the foregoing extracts have been made, a very great number of new veins of gold and silver bearing quartz have been discovered. During the summer of 1867, General James H. Carleton, of the army, who has resided many years in New Mexico, visited some of the mineral regions in that Territory, and wrote a letter for publication, which gives the results of his observation. Here is the letter:

"PINOS ALTOS, NEW MEXICO.

" *To the Editor of the Santa Fé Gazette:*

"It may not be uninteresting to your readers to know something about the town of Pinos Altos, in the southwestern portion of the Territory; a town that is now attracting no little attention from the reports which are circulating that it is the central point of a region very rich in the precious metals. As I have recently made a visit to Pinos Altos, it affords me pleasure to give you for publication the results of my observations and inquiries with reference to the resources of that place, and of the country in its immediate vicinity. On the 15th of last month, Hon. Charles P. Clever, His Excellency Robert B. Mitchell, Captain John Pratt, the Marshal of New Mexico, and myself, left the valley of the Rio Grande at Fort Selden, N. M., where there is a fine ferry, for Fort Cummings, N. M., distant, say, fifty-five miles.

"From Fort Cummings to the Miembres it is eighteen and three-fourth miles. Here the road for Arizona bears off to left, while that for Fort Bayard and Pinos Altos keeps onward, gradually inclining to the right from a west to nearly a northwest course. At about six miles from the Miembres we came to what is known as the Hot Spring. This spring is of a very high temperature, sufficiently so to cook an egg if it be let down into the water where it first comes up out of the earth. The water seems to be highly charged with lime, has some iron in it, and, to a small degree, some salt. There may be other substances in it, but none are abundant enough to render the water unpalatable when it has become cold. The lime which the water has held in solution by an excess of carbonic acid, and by the heat, has been precipitated around the spring in such a quantity, in the way of travertine, as to form a mound some twenty-five feet higher than the surrounding plain. The ascent to the summit of this mound is very gradual. For many ages, doubtless, the water has ceased boiling over the summit, and the travertine becoming more or less decayed, has given way here and there, and allowed it to find small channels through to the outer sides of the slope below the top. These channels have thus drained the spring until the surface of the water has gone down, say, five or six feet. It still has a depth of ten or twelve feet, and a diameter of, say, fifteen feet or more. There is water enough running in all directions from this spring, if carefully husbanded, to irrigate quite a farm. Some nice bathing-rooms have been erected on the northern slope of the mound; and here, also, is quite an extensive adobe residence, with fine rooms for those who come for the benefit of the water. Here, too, corn and hay can be got, and good meals, with a plenty of fresh butter and milk, A gentleman named Mastin keeps this place, and is making here other improvements than those mentioned. It is said that the Indians never come here for water, and that they avoid it as bad medicine. The people living here have considerable stock, but do not seem to fear that it will be stolen from the corrals. No watch is kept over this stock during the night. A mile beyond the hot spring is an abundance of fine, clear, cold water. Thence to Fort Bayard, say seventeen miles, the road is somewhat rough in places from loose stones, but as a general thing it is most excellent. The scenery on either hand, and in front, is of the most charming description, and the air, at you gradually ascend toward the mountains to the northwest, becomes cool and invigorating. One could hardly imagine a more delightful drive than this, from the hot spring to Fort Bayard.

"Fort Bayard, as yet, is only an assemblage of log houses. It has a capacity for some three or four companies. It was intended to build the fort of a more durable material. Some stone foundations, for the permanent quarters, have already been commenced. A post of four companies of cavalry and two of infantry, at this place, would be strong enough soon to drive off or destroy the marauding Apaches, which now are so great an obstacle to the filling up by farmers, stockgrowers, and miners of this important part of New Mexico.

"This post is about half way between the Santa Rita copper mines and the town of Pinos Altos, by roads you are obliged to travel if you are in a carriage. By an air-line, the copper mines are nearest. As the crow flies, Pinos Altos is about eight miles west of Fort Bayard, and the Santa Rita mines are about five miles eastwardly from the post. The Hanover copper mine is about seven miles in an air-line, in a northerly direction from the post. From the summit of the ridge east of the copper mines, and say, three miles distant, to eight or ten miles west of Pinos Altos, there is a belt of country, say thirty miles long, from N. E. to S. W., by ten miles broad, that is *known to be* filled with rich veins of gold, silver, copper, lead, iron, and other metals in combination. Outside of this tract it is believed there is an abundance of mines just as valuable; but that part of the country has not been so carefully examined as the tract here described. The whole of this country is well wooded and covered with fine pasturage, and there are several streams of permanent water upon it. During the rainy season, and for some weeks after it is over, nearly all of the arroyos have more or less of water in them.

"On the 19th of June, we went to Pinos Altos, and staid there until the 22d. We were hospitably entertained by the citizens, and they took every pains to give us all possible information in relation to the town and the mines. The history of the place may be summed up in a few words.

"In May, 1860, a Colonel Snively and a party of California miners came to this region and discovered gold near the present site of the town of Pinos Altos, in what is known as Rich Gulch. In June of that year people commenced coming, to work in *placers*. In December, 1860, there were, say, fifteen hundred here from Chihuahua, Sonora, Texas, and from California. They, at that time, averaged to the hand some ten or fifteen dollars per day. Other gulches were discovered during the fall and summer of 1860. In December, 1860, the first quartz mine was discovered by Mr. Thomas Mastin, with a party of prospecters. This vein is called the Pacific mine; it runs through the hill or mountain, rather, which constitutes the 'divide' of the continent, and has been worked on each slope of that mountain.

"In the spring of 1861, this mine was bought by Mr. Virgil Mastin, a brother of the discoverer, and it was successfully worked during the rest of that year. During 1861, the Apache Indians made formidable raids on the stock of the miners, and nearly stripped them of the means to prosecute their labors. A severe battle was fought between the miners and a band of this tribe, under Mangas Coloradas and Cachces. The Indians numbered about five hundred warriors, and came directly into the town now known as Pinos Altos, which the miners had established in a point central to the scene of their labors. This was on the 27th of September, 1861. Captain Thomas Mastin, who commanded a company of volunteers, was killed in this fight. The Indians were driven off, but the impression they had made on the minds of the inhabitants of the town was so great as to induce the most of the latter to go away. The breaking out of the rebellion also had the effect to induce many to leave. A few only held on, and amongst them was, Mr. Virgil Mastin, who foresaw the future development of the great wealth and promise of this region.

"Not much was done in discovering or in testing the merits of new leads from 1861 to 1864, when still another attempt was made to work the Pacific mine, and a few other mines which Mr. Virgil Mastin had meantime discovered. These latter lodes are known as the Atlantic, Adriatic, and Bear Creek. The work commenced on these had been prosecuted but a short time, when the Apaches again came and stripped the miners of their stock. This caused another suspension of nearly all further labors until 1866, when Mr. Virgil Mastin, Mr. Samuel J. Jones, Mr. Joseph Reynolds, Mr. J. Edgar Griggs, and Mr. Jacob Amberg, organized a company, under the name and style of ' *The Pinos Altos Mining Company*,' under charter granted by the Legislature of New Mexico. This company has three lodes, viz, the Pacific, Atlantic, and Bear Creek. Its stock consists of four hundred shares, at five hundred dollars par value per share, which stock is owned as follows: Virgil Mastin has one hundred and twenty; Samuel J. Jones has sixty; Jacob Amberg has one hundred; Joseph Reynolds has sixty, and J. Edgar Griggs has sixty. None of the shares are for sale. The company has now a steam mill in the town of Pinos Altos, which drives three batteries of five stamps each. When all three batteries are kept at work night and day, they crush twenty tons of ore in twenty-four hours. The average yield of ore extracted from the Pacific mine is from eighty to one hundred and fifty dollars per ton. Ore *can be selected* from this lead which will yield one thousand dollars per ton. This mill is not, as yet, crushing ore taken from the Atlantic and Bear Creek lodes; but ore taken from these has been reduced in arastras, and has yielded as much as ore taken from the Pacific. The Atlantic lies east of Pinos Altos one and a half miles; the Bear Creek half a mile to the south of the town, and the Pacific one and a half miles to the west. On this latter lead or lode a tunnel has already been drifted seven hundred and thirteen feet. Its eastern terminus is on the Atlantic slope of the mountain. Its western terminus, when the tunnel is completed, will debouch upon the Pacific slope. Then the tunnel will be sixteen hundred feet long. Midway it passes under the crest of the mountain, where an air-shaft is run down, which will enter the tunnel one hundred and twenty-one feet below the summit. This tunnel is six and a half feet high, and is five feet wide. A tram-way is laid down upon its floor, and on this is a small car, which carries out the ore as fast as it is mined by the workmen drifting in the tunnel. It costs, to extract ore from the mine, not to exceed six dollars per ton. It costs, delivered at the mill in town, eight dollars and fifty cents. This covers all expenses, including extracting, hauling, &c., &c. The actual expense of crushing this ore is about three dollars per ton.

" The Pacific vein is from three to eleven feet wide, and is inexhaustable. It contains gold, silver, and, in places, a small proportion of copper. The company has nearly completed furnaces for the smelting of the silver ores taken from this mine. These will yield in dollars, per ton, more than the gold ores heretofore alluded to. The cost of smelting siver ores per ton will be twenty-five per cent. less than the cost of crushing the gold ores.

"There are now, within a radius of six miles from the centre of the town of Pinos Altos, over six hundred lodes of gold and silver, as I have been informed by good authority. Several of them prospect equal to those mentioned. Among them are 'The Bear Creek Extension,' owned by Captain William L. Rynerson and company; 'The Santa Juliana,' owned by 'The Bay State Pinos Altos Mining Company;' 'The Montezuma Silver Mine,' owned by Langston and company; 'The Langston Mine,' (silver) owned by Langston and company; 'The Turkey Creek,' 'Weirt,' and 'Aztec,' owned by Mastin, Reynolds and company; 'The Santo Domingo Pinos Altos silver and lead mine;' 'The Perdido Silver Mine,' owned by Davis, Mastin and company; 'The Forest Tree' silver mine, owned by Long Brothers and company; 'Summit,' gold and silver lode, 'Niantic' and 'Indigo,' owned by Rynerson, Stone and company; 'The Aztec No. 2,' owned by Reed, Jones and company; and 'The Mechanics,' and 'The Central,' owned by Owens and company; 'The Extension to Montezuma' and 'The Extension to the Langston,' have been opened up and are owned by Howard, Ward and company; 'The Variety Lode' is owned by William Kness and company. Mr. Houston has also a very rich gold lead, and St. Vrain and company a lead rich in silver and lead. Bates, Cooper and company have also a fine lead near town, called 'The Buckeye.' All of the gentlemen named, and others who have found and perfected their titles to leads at and near Pinos Altos, deserve great credit for their energy and perseverance under the most discouraging circumstances. Now, in all tho gulches, or ravines, which come down from the slopes of the neighboring mountains, the earth is rich in gold, and, in the rainy season, will yield to the hand per day an average of from five to six dollars.

"The population in October, 1866, at the time of renewing operations by the Pinos Altos Mining Company, did not exceed sixty miners. They now number from eight hundred to one thousand, and have erected and are now building some very comfortable dwelling-houses and some commodious stores at Pinos Altos. Here provisions can be bought at reasonable rates. For example: superfine flour can be bought at eleven dollars per sack of one hundred pounds; and bacon, hams, sugar, coffee, &c., at proportionate prices. Most all articles required by miners, such as clothing, tools, blasting-powder, and fuse, &c., &c., can be purchased at moderate prices. The country is well timbered, and the climate unsurpassed in salubrity by any within our boundaries between the two oceans. Pinos Altos is something over five thousand feet above the sea level. It is built exactly on the summit of the great chain of mountains dividing the waters falling into the Atlantic from those falling into the Pacific. As the town increases in size, it will be built down either slope. It is eight miles from Fort Bayard; thirty miles from the Miembres Hot Springs; thirty-six miles from Miembres river; thirteen miles from the Santa Rita copper mines; from Mesilla, on the Rio Grande, one hundred and fifteen miles; from Fort Selden, one hundred and ten miles; from old Fort West, on the Gila river, thirty miles; and from Tucson, Arizona, one hundred and seven.

" Freight can be hauled to Pinos Altos from Mesilla, Las Cruces, and Fort Selden, for two and a-half cents per pound.

" The information I have here given has been gathered from personal observation, and from the statements of those who live at Pinos Altos, and who are persons of credit. It is my opinion, that before six years shall have passed away, there will be a town at or near Pinos Altos larger than the city of Denver. It may be doubted if there is on the known surface of the earth an equal number of square miles on which may be found as many as rich and extensive veins of the useful, as well as of the precious metals, as at and near Pinos Altos, New Mexico. As soon as a few mills demonstrate the real value of even a few of the mines, capital will be sure to drift in that direction to develop them all. It is possible that mills for crushing ores, if erected in large numbers, will, for convenience of water, be built down on Bear creek, or even at the nearest point upon the Gila; but the ores are so rich they will pay the transportation upon a railroad to the Gila river. The whole distance is a 'down' grade. It requires no stretch of the imagination, nor any effort of fancy, to contemplate a time, close at hand, when the smokes of numerous furnaces and the noise of stamp-mills will be seen and heard throughout all this region. The elements of wealth and material prosperity are surely there, and just so soon as those who hold capital can become convinced by actual observation, or by proof gathered from the experience of others, that money invested in quartz-mills, in smelting furnaces, in foundries, and in machine shops, will yield a larger per cent., profit than when loaned on good securities, if put into other branches of trade or industry elsewhere, just that soon will it float to Pinos Altos, and urge forward the development of that region with an energy that will yet surprise even those who have been hopeful of the mineral wealth of New Mexico.

"It was near the end of June when we returned to the Rio Grande. At Fort Selden, at Las Cruces, and at Mesilla, as well as wherever we stopped on our way back to Santa Fé, we met with the greatest kindness and the most generous hospitality. One could hardly imagine a more delightful or interesting journey than that would be to a stranger going from Santa Fé to Las Cruces and Mesilla, and thence to the mineral region at Pinos Altos.

" The Old Placers.

"Four years ago, Governor Connelly, Col. T. Howe Watts, Major DeForrest, and myself, paid a visit to the mines known as the *Old Placer* mines, twenty-seven miles from Santa Fé, New Mexico. We then, after actual inspection, came to the conclusion that the mines themselves were very rich, and could be developed with profit; but we were also as well convinced that the management of the mines owned by the 'New Mexican Mining Company' was intrusted to unskill-

and incompetent heads. A want of system, and a want of an intelligent direction of even what little work was then doing, it was painful to contemplate. We all became fully satisfied that the company was wasting much valuable time, and throwing away a good deal of money to no purpose. Within a year, however, all this has been changed. Now, under a skillful superintendent, who devotes all his time and his ability to demonstrate the truth that the mines which the company had opened are mines that will yield a large profit on the capital invested, the aspect of the affairs of that company has completely changed, and the stock is gradually acquiring a firm and healthy tone in the market. Within the last few days I have repeated my visit to the *Old Placers* in company with Mr. James L. Johnson, one of the leading merchants of New Mexico, and the results of my observations and calculations may not be uninteresting to the people of the Territory.

"With regard to the extent of the mines *already opened* by the New Mexican Mining Company, it may be fairly stated that they are inexhaustible. This company, owns a tract of mineral lands ten miles square; within this area the out-croppings of mines not developed at all are abundant and are of the most promising character. Rising out of the centre of this property are what are known as the Gold mountains. In the lapse of ages these mountains have been grooved by the action of the elements and by the mechanical abrasion of boulders forced downward by ancient torrents, until an inclined plain or *talus*, is formed all around their base, which is rich in what is known as placer gold broken off from the upper crests of gold bearing ledges which must still have existence beneath the present surface. Some of these ledges have been discovered, as before stated, by their out-croppings, and amongst these are those now operated upon by the company. Many are now hidden by soil. These veins have a general direction from north to south. Now, it is therefore reasonable to conclude, from the evidence given of immense wealth in gold in the talus or inclined plain just described, that eventually when these mountains are tunnelled from east to west, that these lodes will all be cut—when they can be successfully attacked far below the surface, and drifted in upon along their entire course. There can likewise be no doubt, that water can be brought from the Pecos river and used as water is used in California to wash, by hose, the most of this auriferous soil and drift which lies around the base of the mountains. In doing this the summits of many new lodes will be uncovered; and when the hydraulic operations no longer remunerate—the water will come there to be used in the far more profitable and steady business of crushing ores from the quartz leads thus brought to light, and from the quartz leads already known which lie above the level to be reached by this water.

"These ideas are briefly given to show what capital and skill will without a doubt eventually accomplish. For the present, it may not be uninteresting to give some statistics showing results to be obtained from the veins already opened.

"The cost of an eighteen horse-power steam engine with fifteen stamps *complete*, put up upon the ground, will be $12,000.

"The cost of a suitable building, to cover this machinery, &c., will be, say, not over $3,000; total $15,000.

"Those who put up the mill should have $5,000 or $10,000 in goods to sell to hands and to people who come to wash placer gold. This contemplates a capital to start on, of from $20,000 to $25,000.

"To run your mill night and day, you want two engineers, whose wages will be four dollars a day, each, including their board. This amounts to $2,920 per annum. You want two feeders at two and a half dollars a day, each, including board, which, per annum, is equal to $1,825. You want two plate tenders, whose wages, each, per day will be two and a half dollars, including board; this is equal to $1,460 per annum. These plate tenders wheel in quartz and shovel the tailings from the vats. You want three cords of wood as fuel for each day of twenty-four hours run. This will cost, delivered, $7 50 per day, or, $2,737 50 per annum. The engineers handle the wood and keep up the fires, so that no firemen need be employed. The cost of lard, tamping, candles, &c., &c., will be, say, $2 50 per day. This is equal per annum to $912 50. The cost of fifty pounds of quicksilver, which would be enough to last a year, would be $75, including losses. The cost of extracting ore is $5 per ton. The freight on the same, delivered at the mill is $2 per ton. The mill will crush nine tons every twenty-four hours. This is equal to three thousand two hundred and eighty-five tons per annum; which, at $7 a ton, delivered at the mill, is equal to $22,995. The wear and tear of machinery and mill is reckoned at five per cent. per annum. I am told by engineers that this is a very liberal allowance. In one year this will amount to $750.

" Recapitulation of annual cost.

Wages of two engineers	$2,920 00
Wages of two feeders	1,825 00
Wages of two plate tenders	1,460 00
Fuel	2,737 50
Lard, tamping, candles, &c., &c	912 50
Quicksilver	75 00
Cost of ore at mill	22,995 00
Interest on cost of mill at 6 per cent	900 00
Wear and tear of mill	750 00
Total cost	$34,575 00

" The following is the result of five small runs through the mill of the New Mexican Mining Company, made by Dr. Michael Steck, the present superintendent:

22 tons yielded per ton	$20 62
16 tons yielded per ton	36 00
16 tons yielded per ton	22 00
6 tons yielded per ton	33 33⅓
3 tons yielded per ton	42 00

" That is to say, sixty-three tons produced $1,707 64; or an average of $27 10 per ton. Much of this ore was refuse ore, which was crushed mainly to get it out of the way. The regular yield of average samples of ore, at the lowest estimate, will be $30 per ton. This, in a year's run, Sundays included, would give $98,550. Now throw off twenty-five per cent. to cover salary of superintendent, delays for the Sabbath, and delays for repairs, and for unforseen contingencies, and you throw off $24,637 50, which will leave $73,912 50. Now deduct from this, expenses of running the mill for a year, as is shown by the recapitulation of annual costs, which is $34,575, and you have clear profit, $39,337 50. This will give on the investment for one year, on cost of mill, which is $15,000—two hundred and sixty-two per cent. For it must be recollected that all other expenses have already been deducted. This does not include the profits on the sale of goods. Two other mills of the same capacity can be erected at two other springs in the hollow where the present mill now stands, and one mill can be erected near what is known as the 'Cunningham mine.' This should be done, when the clear income of the company will be increased to $157,350, which is four times the sum cleared by one mill. This does not include the profit of the store, and yet this gives six per cent. per annum on a capital of $2,622,500. By having the 'cleaning up' in each mill occur on a different day from the cleaning up in any other mill, one superintendent could direct the business transacted by all four mills. The ore is inexhaustible, even in the mines already opened. Other mines on this ten miles square can be opened, and there are *known* springs where still other mills can be erected. By a system of tanks and reservoirs to collect and hold surface water, any number of mills can be run, and all this without making any calculations for water coming from the Pecos. When there is so much material to be worked upon with profit, to have but one mill, is the same as if you had a boundless supply of cotton, and worked upon it with a factory running fifteen spindles.

" I have taken some little pains to prove to you by figures, that here within sight of the city of Santa Fé, there is a fund of wealth which bespeaks well for the future prosperity of *this* part of New Mexico. I have written nothing of the *New Placers*, which are known to be equally as rich and extensive; nor have I alluded to the auriferous region in the mountains to the west of Mr. Maxwell's ranch, on the Cimarron river. Should I have time to visit and properly examine these two last named placers, it will give me pleasure to let you know the result of my observation.

"When the vast mineral, pastoral, and even agricultural resources of New Mexico are well understood, it will require no prophet to foresee that she will, one day, not far distant, occupy a proud position as one of the States of the great Republic.

"Very respectfully, your obedient servant,

"JAMES H. CARLETON.

After having written this letter, General Carleton visited what are known as the *New Placers*, south of the *Old Placer* described in the foregoing letter. What is called the San Pedro grant includes the mineral region known as the *New Placer*. It contains forty thousand acres, and lies about forty miles south of the city of Santa Fé. It is accessible by excellent roads. Mining at the *New Placer*, we know, was carried on as early as 1776. I give an extract from a letter descriptive of the *New Placer*:

"METROPOLITAN HOTEL,
" *Washington, D. C., October* 18, 1867.

" GENERAL : * * * I visited the *New Placers* in November, 1865, and again in August of this year. Since my first visit several new lodes have been discovered, and I was informed by prospectors that in nearly every part of the grant—which comprises, as I learn, some forty thousand acres—lodes of gold-bearing quartz and of argentiferous galena, as well as veins of lead and of copper of a rich character, can be found. I saw some exceedingly rich copper ore from a newly discovered vein on this property. I have seen tested some quartz taken from recently discovered lodes at the *New Placers*, and found it to be rich in gold. You may recollect that I sent some specimens which I took from the Ramirez mine to Colonel Carey, and that I wrote to him a letter about that particular mine. I have seen quartz crushed

at the *Old Placers*, and in July, of this year, I made some calculations as to its value, which calculations appeared in the
Santa Fé Gazette on the 27th of that month.   Now it is my
opinion that the *Ramirez mine* is even richer, per ton, than
the *Ortiz mine*, from which that quartz was taken.   *   *   *
On the south side of the Old Placer mountains, and close to
the line of the *New Placer*, some gold mines have been found,
which, even at the surface, produced fifty-three dollars per
ton.   Mr. Hutchinson, who is developing these mines, informed me that over the line, and within the boundaries of
the *New Placer*, he had found new lodes of auriferous quartz
just as rich.   I have no hesitation in expressing the opinion
that within our whole country, so far as my observation has
extended, a piece of ground of the size of the *New Placers*
cannot be found which contains more or richer veins of the
precious metals than it does; and I would recommend that
good mills be at once erected for their extraction.   As soon
as the Pacific railroad is built, and the surveys indicate that
it will run immediately by the *New Placers*, it is impossible
to conjecture how greatly that grant will be increased in
value.   The grant, as you are aware, is uncommonly well
wooded, and even for grazing purposes, is equal to any in
New Mexico.

"I am, general, very truly yours,
"JAMES H. CARLETON.
"General JOHN C. McFERRAN,
"*U. S. Army, Washington, D. C.*"

About the middle of July, 1867, some gold fields were
discovered on the head waters of the little Cimarron, between Maxwell's ranch and the Taos valley; say thirty miles
west of Mr. Maxwell's.   These promise to yield *placer* gold
in great abundance.   A party of gentlemen visited these
fields in the month of August last.   One of them wrote to
me: "The *placers* were just beginning to be opened.   The
miners had but few tools, and were experiencing great difficulty in getting lumber to make sluices.   One company of
five men with a sluice ninety feet long were taking out seven

hundred dollars in gold per week, others were just commencing, and were realizing less, but a fair remuneration, considering the poor appliances they had with which to work. By October 1867, the company of five above alluded to were taking out one hundred dollars apiece per day," * * * "Of course all do not do as well, but experiments made by prospectors show that the fields are many miles in extent." One company is now constructing a ditch or canal to bring water upon portions of these fields. This ditch will cost $100,000, and yet the parties interested in its construction are certain soon to be reimbursed for all their out-lay.

A town has been laid out near the principal washings; it is called "Virginia City," and will without doubt soon be a place of much importance. There is hardly a day that *new* discoveries of gold are not made in that portion of New Mexico."

If Congress will only give some help to these hard working men, by constructing a good wagon road from Maxwell's ranch to Virginia city, and it can be done for the small sum of thirty or forty thousand dollars, all kinds of supplies can be readily got in at cheap rates; when more and more poor people will flock thither, and will soon give back to the Government, in return, the gold now so much needed.

This is no chimera. *We know its reality.* All we want is a little help here and there, until we in New Mexico can get a start, *then* the country will see that we can help others as well as ourselves.

The *placers*, or gold fields, near Virginia city have become rich from the disintregation of gold-bearing quartz veins in the mountains east, and in the range of mountains west of the extensive valley in which they lie. This valley is called the Moreño pass, and the fields are called the Moreño mines. Many of the lodes whence this gold has come have not yet been uncovered; but that they exist near these fields is as certain as that a spring exists whence a rivulet flows. All along the cordilleras of the Rocky Mountains, extending from the Moreño mines northward to Pike's Peak, in Colorado; on each slope of them are found *placer* diggings. On the Rio

3

Grande side of the mountains at the Hondo, near Taos; at the Culebra, near Fort Garland; at the Saugre de Christo, near the pass of that name, gold has been found in paying quantites. On the east side, as well, prospectors have found good *placers* from the Raton mountains to the Rincon de Tecolote.

Near the Moreño mines, high up a neighboring mountain, is one of the richest copper mines in the world. A company consisting of Mr. William II. Moore, Lucian B. Maxwell, William Kroenig, Nicholas S. Davis, and others, are drifting through the mountain far below the outcropping of this lode. They have already run a gallery six feet wide by seven feet high, through the solid rock, to a distance of over two hundred feet; and expect, within another hundred feet, to strike the main vein, when countless tons of the ore can be dropped down from above, and be easily run out on a tram-way and taken to furnaces for smelting.

In the Tejeras cañon, near Albuquerque, several very rich leads of copper have been discovered, and a company has procured from the Territorial Legislature a charter for working them. The ore from these mines is of the very best quality, whilst water and fuel in abundance, for necessary smelting purposes, are just at hand.

The Nacimiento Mining Company, also chartered by the Legislature, has an abundance of copper ores, yielding from sixty-three to seventy-one per cent. These mines are at the head-waters of the Puerco river, near Abiquiu. Gold is also found near Embudo, and here there is a vein of silver ore of great promise. It is called the Junction Lead. Near this point are extensive lodes of iron; and cinnabar is found in large quantities near Las Truches, on the trail from Santa Fé to Taos.

In the Sierra de los Ladrones, near Limitar, as well as in the San Andres mountains, north of the San Augustine pass, silver lodes of great size, are known to exist. So, too, in the Sacramento mountains, south of Fort Stanton, gold, silver, and lead, have been found; but, owing to the hostilities of the *Mescalero Apaches*, prospectors have not yet been able satisfactorily to explore the lodes.

In the Zuñi mountains, near Fort Wingate, and in many places in the old Navajoe country, gold and silver have been discovered; and, from surface indications, it is believed that very rich lodes are there.

Thus it will be seen by a glance at the map that, in nearly every quarter of that extensive Territory, the mineral wealth heretofore hidden beneath the earth's surface has been tracked to its bed. And now the people of New Mexico, with as much propriety as those in California, can honestly and earnestly exclaim " we have found it."

We now come to the inquiry: " Why do not the people of New Mexico themselves develop their gold and silver and copper leads?" Let me answer.

We have in that Territory a population of, say, in round numbers, one hundred thousand souls. Of these, say fifteen thousand are Pueblo Indians and Indians on a reservation. The mass of the people are very poor. The most of the prospectors are expert in the business of prospecing and are mainly discharged soldiers who belonged to the California volunteers. During their term of service, whilst on campaigns against Indians, and whilst marching from one point to another of the Territory, they saw indications of its riches. So, when the time came for their discharge, a great many of them preferred to remain in New Mexico rather than to return to California. It was then that a new impetus was given to the prospecting of the country in search of its hidden mines. The results have startled with their greatness the most sanguine and enthusiastic believer that gold and silver abounded in large quantities in that Territory.

Let us take the labors of one prospector as an example. With what little money he had saved up in his military service, the soldier has bought a few tools, and, perhaps, a mule, or pony, a rifle, and a sack of flour, some bacon, sugar, coffee, and salt. In portions of the country, where the Indians were very bad, several of these prospectors would join together in their searches; when there was but little or no danger, they would sally forth alone, camping out wherever night overtook them. A lode is found and the miner at once sinks a hole in the quartz to procure specimens to test its value. These specimens are crushed by pounding with a hammer until they are as fine as flour. This quartz-flour is then washed in a large horn spoon, the particles of gold being the heaviest, gradually go to the bottom, whilst the particles of quartz are allowed to pass off over the edge of the spoon. Shortly nothing is left but the gold. We will suppose that the vein has proved to be rich. Then the law requires that certain steps should be taken—a certain amount of labor be peformed—certain surveys be made, and, finally, if no one contests the miner's right to his discovery, he can get a patent from the Government, and the mine is his, as much as a farmer's farm is his when he has got his deed for it. I may say, in passing, that new legislation should be had on this subject, simplifying the mode by which a poor man can get his patent, and making it shorter as to time, and cheaper as to money.

The prospector has now found his mine, and has got his title to it. It may yield at the rate of twenty, thirty, forty, fifty, eighty, or more dollars to the ton, and be inexhaustible in extent. He is a rich man, one might suppose. Not so; he is still poor, and has to go off somewhere and labor even for his daily bread. Now, the example here given is that of hundreds of miners who have found hundreds of mines they *know* to be good. It takes *capital* to buy and bring machinery to crush this quartz and save the gold. But why do not people with capital do this? Because, as yet, the country is not made accessible by railroad. Wealthy men will not make the journey unless they can travel rapidly and with ease and security; and the poor miner, like the Pueblo Indian, who turns to the east every morning, hoping to see, coming thence, the divine form of Montezuma, so does he turn his eyes in the same direction, and pray for the day when the rich man with his money will come to be a partner with the poor man with his mine.

If a private citizen owned a fine lot of trees worth a million of dollars if gotten to market, and it would cost him five thousand dollars to make a road suitable to the getting of them out of the forest, so that he could make sale of them, would he not even *borrow* money, if necessary, to raise this five thousand dollars? Certainly he would. Well, now, the United States have locked up, in these quartz veins in New Mexico, millions of the precious metals. Every man *to-day* is paying thirty or forty cents on the dollar merely for the want of these metals. Think of that sum! Yet the *nation* does not seem to be alive to its interests as the private citizen would be to his; and goes on, and on, and on, forgetting the hardship to especially the poor who for lack of gold, with scanty means, have to pay high prices for the necessaries of life; forgetting the enterprising yet poor miner, he who has here been figured, waiting for *his* Montezuma; forgetting the employment which it would give to many of its brave defenders who in vain now seek labor; forgetting that at once when a railroad runs through New Mexico, a hundred dollars will come back where one dollar has been invested, and yet the logic which would convince a private citizen what he should do to increase his wealth, ought to hold good, if starting from the same premises, with the country at large.

I make some extracts from a letter written from the office of the Union Pacific Railway, which touch directly upon the matter under consideration.

"Our preliminary surveys of the present summer have discovered a favorable line to this point, whose highest elevation at the head of Cañon Blanco, in latitude 35° north, 60 miles east of Albuquerque, is 7,136 feet above the level of the sea. By these surveys, necessarily preliminary and less minute than those of definite location, a practicable route for railroad construction was found, avoiding heavy gradients and expensive grading, and requiring the maximum grade permitted by law for the Pacific railroads at only two or three short intervals, not exceeding twenty-five miles in all. The distance from Pond creek to Albuquerque, by the preliminary survey, is 464 miles, or from the initial point of our road on the Missouri river to the Rio Grande at Albuquerque, 872 miles, which may be reduced upon the definite location of the road. From Albuquerque, surveys, by the 35th parallel and the Gila river, through Arizona and thence to San Francisco, are now in progress, and favorable accounts of the routes traversed have been received from the engineering parties. It is expected that these surveys will reach San Francisco early in February, this company will be in full possession of the topographical features of the country examined by its engineers.

" The route across the divide of the waters of the Smoky hill and Arkansas rivers, is chiefly valuable for grazing purposes; but, upon reaching the valley of the Arkansas, vast regions are opened for settlement, which, for varied productions—embracing all the cereals, fruit and grapes—are nowhere surpassed. The salubrity and healthfulness of the climate, and the abundance of coal and timber, make it the most agreeable unocupied country in the United States; and when to these advantages are added the certainty of the production of the precious metals, in amounts hitherto unknown, no region can be more desirable, or more profitably developed; and so the country alternates all the way to the Rio Grande, no portion valueless, but all adapted to grazing or agriculture; and, as regards the mineral wealth along the route thither, it may be safely said that the amount is only limited by the labor bestowed in its development.

" Having thus briefly designated the route upon which the company requests extension of subsidy, I will ask your attention to a concise enumeration of the resources of the country to be traversed, with their present known development, and the probability of their immense increase when quick and cheap rail transportation is afforded. Crossing the Raton mountain, and entering the Territory of New Mexico, our geologist discovered in the single coal deposit near Maxwell's hacienda, fifty miles northeast of Fort Union, veins of bituminous coal extending for a range of sixty miles, one of which, on Vermijo cañon, was ten feet in thickness, and was examined for an area of ten miles square. This coal, when analyzed by Messrs Williams and Moss, analytical chemists of Philadelphia, Pennsylvania, yielded 53.90 per cent. of fixed carbon alone, and produced 437.6 lbs. of illuminating gas per ton of 2,000 lbs., equivalent to 7439.2 cubic feet. These chemists report this coal to compare very favorably with any of those regarded as the best for generating steam, and with the majority of those used for manufacturing illuminating gas. Anthracite coal is found in the Placer mountain, near Santa Fé; bituminous coal on the west side of the Rio Grande, near Albuquerque; and very extensive coal beds farther south on that river near Fort Craig. So successful have been our researches for coal supplies, that our chief engineer characterizes the New Mexican coal fields as 'the great natural depot of fuel, not only for this Pacific railway, but for the country contiguous to it, for, at least, as far east as Fort Harker, Kansas.' And there can be no doubt that our discoveries of the past summer alone have eliminated the fuel question from the obstacles or embarrassments of a railway across the continent, and made its ample fuel supply no longer problematical.

" The great expense of transporting the heavier and more effective quartz-crushing machinery across the eight hundred miles of wagon roads between the mines and railway, have heretofore nearly restricted New Mexican mining to placer working; the exception has been the cheaper, though less effective, modes of quartz milling. In this rude and unproductive manner, the mines of New Mexico have been worked for more than two centuries, adding large supplies to the demands of commerce. The ores of that Territory are of a most favorable character for easy and cheap reduction, and are inexhaustible. The company has the most conclusive evidence of this fact. It is asserted by those who have had good means of acquiring the knowledge, that the mines of Arizona are richer, and, with railroad facilities, would be more productive than any and all yet wrought upon the continent. The explorations of the company have not progressed sufficiently to enable it to verify the assertion to the fullest extent, but, so far as it has received information thereon, the mines are astonishingly rich.

"An abundance of native Mexican and Pueblo labor exists in New Mexico and Arizona, which can be made available immediately upon the passage of the bill, and by mingling with our own labor under proper direction, a healthy industry will be developed, and the native artisans instructed, Christianized and prepared for useful citizenship. That this labor can be maintained without requiring supplies from the States, and is adequate to building at least five hundred miles through these Territories, were considerations which strongly recommended this projected route to the company. And with the labor indigenous to the soil, the presence of iron ore and the coal with which it may be wrought, must necessarily induce the erection of factories and furnaces in New Mexico and Arizona, where now only the miner's ranche is seen. Capital will find useful and lucrative employment, and every branch of industry, co-operative with the work of construction, speedy development, peopling the present wilderness in a day. And as these mines of gold and silver become known and successfully worked, how vast will be their influence upon the national currency, to say nothing of the creation of other wealth from trade and commerce. The company believes that the construction of its road would give security to the inhabitants of the Territories of New Mexico and Arizona against the Indians, the necessity for which, as regards those recently located south of the Arkansas, is apparent, while the proposed line of road seems to it admirably adapted to that purpose."

Then, aside from the impetus which a railroad would give to the development of the minerals of New Mexico and Arizona, a thought comes in here, that the red man *must* give way before the iron-horse, as the army of Assyria perished when breathed upon by the angel of death; and when once the Indian ceases his depredations, the flocks and herds of New Mexico, Colorado, Texas, and Arizona will become so numerous as to afford mutton and beef to the poor all over the country at vastly cheaper rates. So you will increase the value of a day's labor, by making money more valuable, when compared with the price of food. This may be an exception to some of the rules of political economy, but it is true nevertheless.

I quote from a very interesting paper on the Union Pacific Railway, the following remarks about cattle raised in Texas and driven up to a station on that road: **Bancroft Library**

"The cattle here are grazing all over this magnificent valley under the care of herders. The drovers usually herd after arrival from thirty to sixty days to recruit the animals before selling. And such pasturage! The steer that would not fat here visibly would have starved to death in the garden of Eden. But just look at them as they wade in the grass, and see their Fulton market roundness and glossiness. With difficulty I credit the statement that there are 25,000 head here now, waiting shipment. Yet here they are, and 10,000 more are known to be on the way here, and full 50,000 will have arrived at the close of the season. Four times as many would have been driven here as have been, if the stock-men of the southwest had known that there was a safe and sure way out from the lock-up which the war first, and toll-demanding ruffians afterward, had established. So say the most intelligent of these Texan drovers, and they also say that 200,000 head of beeves will surely be here next year for sale and shipment. Now mark: These animals, 'beeves,' can be bought by thousands in Texas at from $8 to $10 per head in gold, or $12 to $14 in currency. They can be driven to Abilene at an additional cost of not over $2 a head, in from five to eight weeks' time. They can be shipped from here to St. Louis at $100 a car load, and to Chicago for $150 a car. Joseph McCoy tells me that they can be afforded in Chicago at four cents gross, with satisfactory margins to drovers, shippers, and railroads. Surely the butchers of more than one city and State have got to come down, and surely there was grateful reason in the toast the Union Pacific railway, eastern division, as the cheapener of beef to the people of the United States."

These remarks would have the same force when applied

to the flocks and herds of New Mexico. "He is a benefactor who makes one blade of grass grow where none grew before." So, too, that government is far seeing which shapes its policy so that its poor can have a plenty of good, wholesome food at cheap rates; which for ten cents will put into the kettle of the poor man two pounds of beef, when for the same sum he could before only find one pound. The government which *can* do this, and *does* do it, is as a benign mother providing for her children. The statesmen who lose sight of such matters now will neither benefit the community at large nor write their names in capitals on the scroll, where already have been inscribed the names of those whom *the people* venerate.

Pertinent to this matter, I find a very interesting letter in the Cincinnati Times, of the 8th instant. It was written by Mr. Edgar Conkling, and it gives me pleasure here to reproduce many of Mr. Conklings conclusive arguments:

"CINCINNATI, *January* 6, 1868.

"MR. EDITOR: The very general reference by the press of our country to the suffering condition of our 'working men and women' from want of employment, arouses our sympathies and warrants the serious consideration of our manufacturers, business men, and all good citizens, how to restore our national industry to a state of prosperity? How shall we materially increase the consumption of the products of American labor, as well as protect them from foreign products? It is encouraging to know that Congress appreciates such a deplorable condition of our most important interests, and is giving some evidence of adopting a financial policy that will encourage capitalists to engage in the construction of railroads from important commercial and manufacturing cities, through sections of country warranting speedy and profitable returns.   *   *   *   *   *

.."But the disturbance of the national industry is too general to be materially affected by mere local projects, while it is admitted that, in many branches, our manufacturing facilities of production are greater than our country can consume;

hence the loss in such investments, while our mechanics and laboring people are being demoralized and suffering for the necessaries of life.

" In a great measure, this state of things is the result of the recent rebellion, and protracted reconstruction. Hundreds of thousands of our happy and well-to-do 'working men' left their occupations to maintain the Government, while others were employed in manufacturing war materials, and thus our national industry was generally disturbed.

" No government on earth can so readily restore its national industry to prosperity as this. None were ever under greater obligations to its citizens. No subjects more faithful, or worthy of needed aid. No reason exists for protracting this state of affairs, unless from lack of statesmanship and interest in our servants in Congress assembled.

" Our Government is possessed of an undeveloped territory, unsurpassed for climate and latent wealth, which, on being opened by national highways, will reach and mature a Pacific commerce much greater than all our Atlantic commerce.

" It has enterprising capitalists, desirous and ready to improve that territory, and make it productive of taxes, soon exceeding all the aid loaned by the Government. Ordinarily, it is difficult to enlist capitalists in such public works, and it is fortunate for our Government, at the present time, that such foreseeing the great and certain benefits that must speedily result to themselves, the Government, and the people, are willing to risk their means, credit, and reputation.

" They simply ask the Government to loan them, well secured, not exceeding one-third the cost of such roads, making that territory worth twenty fold its present value, while giving the Government cheaper facilities of governing and transportation.

" Such aid by the Government is the only practicable and legitimate method of securing such facilities of transportation, and creating and controlling the Pacific commerce.

" Those distant agricultural lands are worthless, only as they are connected by railroads with the mines; with cheap food and transportation for miners, the increased products of the mines of the precious metals will keep pace with our growing wealth and commercial wants, and warrant a safe return to specie payments. But there are large sections of rich mineral lands destitute of fuel and water, and hence cannot have reduction facilities, that will be dependent on shipping their ores, by railroads, for reduction, itself creating a large revenue to the railroads, while redeeming the wealth of such sections, otherwise worthless.

"The advantages claimed are worthy of consideration in the most prosperous times. But in view of our national obligations to our workingmen and their condition, and the depression of our manufacturing interests, and the necessity of making that territory share in our taxes and payment of our public debt, there should be no hesitancy on the part of Congress to promote our National interests. It should be done in view of reciprocating the obligations of the Government to a people that maintained it when assailed by traitors, even if, in spending one hundred millions of dollars there were no other returns but gratefulness for an act of justice.

"Never was there so much of necessity for a mutual union of labor and capital. Both are suffering for want of that union. Mere demagogues will seek to prevent it, but workingmen's logic is sharpened from the want of food, and they will readily discover the motives of those seeking their votes.

"Our territory and national wants, as well as our Pacific commerce, need the three Pacific railroads—North, Central, and Southern—and their healthful competing influence.

"The three trunk lines will cost, at least, $450,000,000, single track, and not exceeding one-third of that amount is asked as a loan of the Government in its bonds, secured by the whole, as the route progresses. So far as the roads have now progressed, the Government has profited beyond the aid loaned, while the companies are doing a business warranting their ability to meet the interest and debt as it matures.

"But if the 'penny-wise and pound-foolish' idea must prevail, that the Government can't afford to increase its indebtedness for such purposes and returns, Senator Ramsey's proposition is worthy of consideration, of asking Congress to guarantee the interest of five per cent. on the stock or bonds of the railroad companies, to the amount of $20,000, per mile for a limited time, which, on 2,000 miles west of Lake Superior, would be a guarantee of five per cent. on $40,000,000, or only $2,000,000 per annum, the company meeting the interest from sales of its lands, business and services for the Government.

"This form of aid would enable that company to borrow the needed funds, while the use of that road to the Government would be more than equal to such interest, to say nothing of advanced value of the territory and our commerce.

"The aid can, and should be afforded, in some shape.

"Hundreds of thousands of our 'workingmen' will thus be benefitted in various ways. Some will be engaged in making the road beds, buildings, &c., and others in making the construction and materials, and running machinery for transporting, &c. But all this is but the beginning of larger outlays to which the Government is not asked to contribute. The whole must be kept in repair. Double tracks and branch roads, increased machinery, &c., all exceeding first outlays, in a few years. Cities, towns, farms, mines, mills, &c., are but results, and will create a greater outlay, than cost of the railroads. This vast increased consumption of products of American labor, will tend greatly to equalize and restore to prosperity our national industry, greatly increasing our national wealth, and ability to support the Government and pay its debt. If this is all true, is it not the interest and the duty of all citizens to urge on Congress immediate action?

"If the measure succeeds satisfactory to capitalists, contracts for all that is needed will speedily follow, materially affecting our general interests."

A volume could be written showing the truth of these remarks; and not one line to prove them to be fallacies. Whatever other roads may be built, the laws of climate will make that which should run through New Mexico the most agree-

able to the traveller and the most certain to meet the demands of trade. It requires but little forecast, and study of
the commercial necessities of the world, to see very nearly
where the great arteries of railroad communication must
pulsate across our continent. There can be no question but
that one line must eventually run westward from Memphis,
to San Diego, California, or to a porton the Gulf of California, which latter, if we cannot acquire it by purchase, we
can have access to it by the comity of a sister republic.
That line will run across the rich mineral region now rapidly
developing in the southern portion of New Mexico. Nor can
there be a doubt, that another line will run somewhere near
the 35th parallel of latitude. To connect these two by a track
in the valley of the Rio Grande will be found not only to be
profitable, but necessary. Here then you have an outline of
a railroad system in this great territory, an outline that will
be filled in by other roads, to be projected by more local interests. And the heavy trains, freighted with the costly products of China, Japan, and Hindostan, can be shot along
these roads with no obstruction from ice and snow. Then
will come that proud day for New Mexico, so often predicted
and now so near realization. In room, then, of being isolated
from the commerce of the world, and from the hourly intelligence which elsewhere now flashes along the wires of the
telegraph, she will be in the direct channels of that commerce and of that intelligence.

I have said nothing of the *hot* springs and of the *mineral*
springs of New Mexico. These are found in almost every
section of the country. At Las Vegas; near Taos; at Ojo
Caliente; at Jemez; near Fort McRae; near Fort Selden;
near the Miembres river, and at many other points. Their
curative qualities have long been known, and the poor as
well as the rich, who may happen to be infirm, flock to them
with almost the same faith that they will find relief, as those
who " when the waters were troubled," descended into the
Pool of Bethsaida. Once the railroad touches New Mexico,
these springs, which for volume and medicinal qualities exceed any of those now so celebrated in the Atlantic States,

or in Europe, will attract thousands from all points of the civilized world to drink of their healing waters. And, then, in room of having tourists go from our own country to spend their money in sight-seeing abroad, they will visit and wonder at the magnificence of this American Switzerland; whilst the wealthy of other lands, from beyond *both* seas, will become tourists in *our* mountains, here to have their villas and their chateaux; here to breathe the pure air, and to enjoy the most sublime scenery to be found in the world. The Genii in the Eastern Tale could never have been more potent in their works of enchantment than Capital and Labor will be, when giving to New Mexico, as the fruit of their union, a railroad to connect her with the commerce of the two oceans, and make her known to the wealthy and cultivated throughout the world.

CHARLES P. CLEVER.